Nickel Plate
Color Photography
of Willis A. McCaleb

Volume 1:
BUFFALO - BELLEVUE

By
Bruce K. Dicken and James M. Semon

Copyright © 1995
Morning Sun Books, Inc.
All rights reserved. This book may not be reproduced in part or
in whole without written permission from the publisher, except in
the case of brief quotations or reproductions of the cover for the
purposes of review.

Published by
Morning Sun Books, Inc.
11 Sussex Court
Edison, NJ 08820
Library of Congress Catalog Card No. 95-079970
First Printing
ISBN 1-878887-52-1

Dedication

To Norma T. McCaleb, Willis' wife who has been the inspiration for this book.

Acknowledgements

This book is the fulfillment of a dream to publish an all color record of the Nickel Plate Road that could be enjoyed
by former Nickel Platers, railfans, historians and modelers. We especially want to thank Bob Lorenz, a close friend,
who first made us aware of the potential that existed in Willis' outstanding slide collection. Bob Yanosey met with us
in March of 1994 to review Willis' slides and enthusiastically encouraged us to move forward with two color books
on the Nickel Plate. He has provided excellent direction for all aspects of this project and we thank him for his assis-
tance. We also want to thank Amanda Dicken for producing many variations of the manuscript on her word processor.
Our families have supported us from the beginning and we wish to thank them for their patience and understanding.

Enjoy the full spectrum of fine, all-color books from Morning Sun

WILLIS A. McCALEB
PHOTO-JOURNALIST

Willis just stepped out of the cab of Hudson 175 in East Cleveland, OH 1958. (Photo: Bob Blatt)

THE NICKEL PLATE AND ME, ALONG THE LINE

I lived for many years on a dead-end street in east Lakewood about 600 feet from the Nickel Plate Road which became a visible and audible background to my life. Before I could even read, I could tell whether an approaching train was eastbound or westbound, passenger, freight or a switch run, simply by the sound even when inside our house.

A low fence stood at the end of the street near the tracks. On many sunny afternoons, I stood watching an 0-6-0 switching the two small industries served by a siding, a trailing switch off the westbound track. Garfield School, two and a half blocks away, had a yard abutting the railroad, so my appreciation of NKP continued during the six years I was in the elementary grades. When I went to Emerson Junior High, it was necessary to cross the tracks each morning and afternoon for three years. When high school came along, the Nickel Plate was about a half mile away, but I could still hear the trains at times.

There was more. The New York Central lakefront line was about a mile to the south, but heard especially loud when a south wind came our way. There were three lines of the Cleveland Railway, one 200 feet from us, and the other two one-half mile, one of which carried the Lake Shore Electric Railway. To add to the cacaphony, the Cuyahoga River and its entry into Lake Erie were a little more than four miles, within easy hearing of tugs and Great Lakes freighters.

Perhaps now, you can understand why I was hooked on transportation. When World War II came, I saw new places, countries and somber events. On my return home, I found a job with the Chesapeake & Ohio Railway. In six years there, I learned about research and the official side of railroading. Then Nickel Plate offered me a job as a photographer.

There after followed 12-1/2 very busy years, the last half or dozen or so which is the subject of this book. At first, the work was mainly for the company magazine and annual report, but it became obvious that there were other needs, so I began to do commercial work for most of the departments, legal evidence work and many visual aid assignments for the Safety and Freight Claim Prevention office. Here, I came to know more about the physical operation and why and how things worked. It was exciting and instructive work, which I fully enjoyed, especially working with and getting to know people and often to help them in their work.

The 1964 merger with Norfolk & Western brought less and less opportunity to use and exercise my individuality. This would turn out to be the close of railroading for me. Nickel Plate was a fine railroad with a conservative, yet innovative attitude toward conducting transportation. With meager plant, it consistently outperformed several much larger railroads. It was fascinating and very satisfying to be involved in and part of such an organization of determined people.

Willis A. McCaleb
July 4, 1995

Tickets for

OUR READERS

... on the NICKEL PLATE ROAD

PREFACE

Anyone living in the 1950's has an opinion about what was right or wrong with the decade. If you were employed by a railroad, or were interested in the trains you rode or watched, those 10 years are precious memories. Our story is about a railroad professional that not only worked for the company, but enjoyed watching and, fortunately for us, photographing the trains.

Safety Car II rests on a siding in March 1959. This was converted in 1953 from Pullman "East Berkshire".

Willis A. McCaleb, also known as Bill, was photographer for the Nickel Plate Road from 1952 until after the merger with Norfolk and Western. This volume tells his story with color transparencies. His slide camera often covered the same assignments done with black and white photos. He documented everything from new locomotives to retirement parties, and this turned out to be a busy time for both.

The Nickel Plate Road (New York, Chicago and St. Louis) ran between Buffalo and Chicago. There were never many branch lines, but during the 1920's, the road took over the Lake Erie and Western and the Clover Leaf. This provided access to Indianapolis, Peoria, and St. Louis. 1949 brought acquisition of the Wheeling and Lake Erie and the Southern Ohio coal fields. New industries and new markets became the symbols of Nickel Plate success.

When Willis joined the company, the switch from steam locomotion to the diesel electric was well underway. His personal interest in trains drove him to capture the fading steam scene, but still to record a forward looking Nickel Plate with new engines and new facilities. It truly was a time of transition.

Willis will take us on a rail journey behind Lima Berkshires, Mikados and steam switchers. All the new diesels are here, including the Alco Bluebirds, still very much in charge of all passenger movements. Willis will also introduce us to some old friends, people he knew and enjoyed, people who made the Nickel Plate a legend.

So let's climb aboard No. 9 for one last run into the night, down the Clover Leaf to St. Louis, or pull up to a grade crossing and witness the final drama of doubleheaded 700's in full cry across the flatlands.

4

Too many lunch pails and lanterns. A safety shot to illustrate the wrong way to descend an Alco yard switcher. Cleveland yards in October 1959.

TABLE OF CONTENTS

On board a Nickel Plate business car in 1963. An official ignores the passing landscape and scans the financial page. Merger is a year away.

Signal maintainer cleans the lenses on the signal at Dover Center Road in Bay Village, OH. This is September 1958.

First generation Hi-cube 38000 just completed at the Greenville Steel Car Co., Greenville, PA in November 1963.

Good housekeeping aboard a GP9 with the crew duffel bags and a faithful broom.

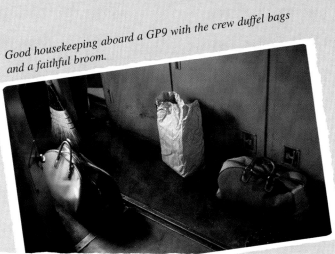

Engineer checks the time on the Cleveland-bound Saucer out of Buffalo. He is anxious to move the freight on this April day in 1959.

Brewster Yard on the Wheeling District provided repairs to rolling stock. In April 1959 the car end is being pulled into place.

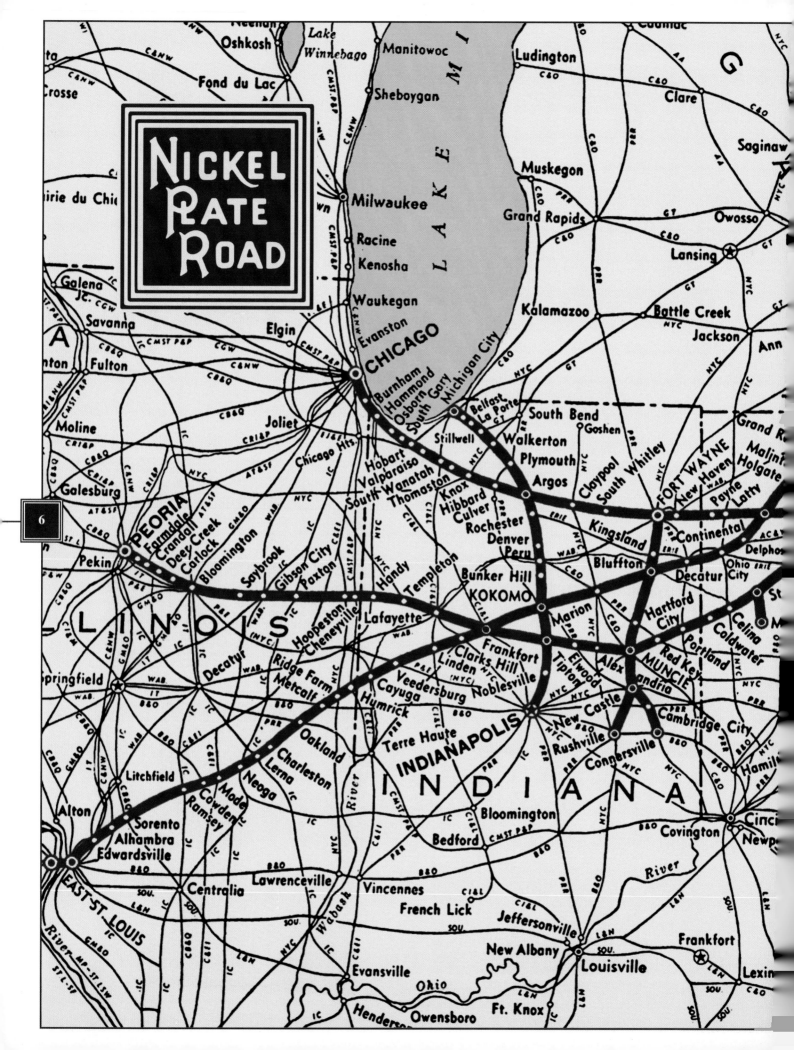

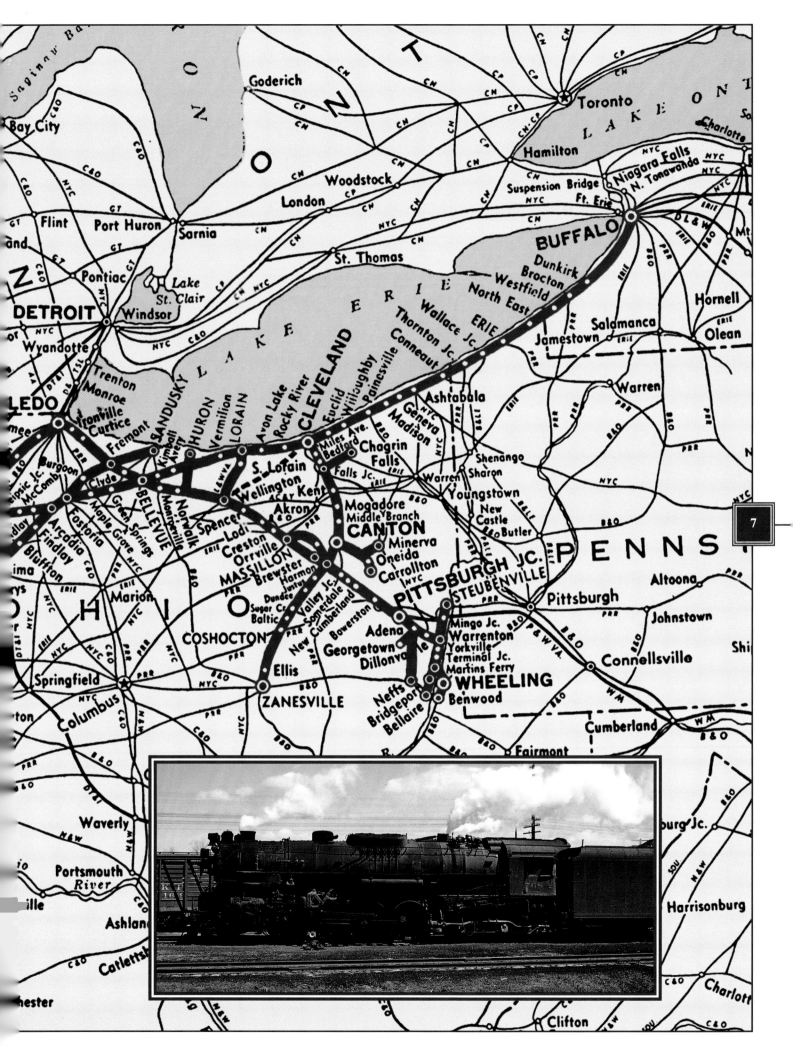

A HUDSON'S FAREWELL

(Above) *The late fifties provided few opportunities to experience a last look at main line steam locomotives. Nickel Plate L-1b Hudson 175 provided one such farewell on May 18, 1958. The Buffalo Chapter of the National Railway Historical Society had chartered a fan trip to Cleveland. Here, Dunkirk, NY, provides a setting for the regal 175 as several fans get a closer look at a Hudson in action.*

(Below) *Thoroughbred 175 has cut off the excursion, and is running for service in Conneaut.*

Engineer Carl Childs brought the special in from Buffalo. He is shown here in front of the engine, along with his fireman. This was not just another day at work; they had just brought a Nickel Plate Hudson into town for the last time.

Willis bought a pair of coveralls in Lakewood to ride the engine. He didn't wash them for 20 years in order to keep some original Nickel Plate soot. After he climbed down from the cab in Conneaut, Myron Phipps, President of the Nickel Plate, spotted him exclaiming, "Hi Bill, how the hell did you get so dirty?" It was the only time Willis rode a steam passenger engine, and his last NKP steam ride.

CORRECTED TO JULY 1, 1928

NICKEL PLATE
ROAD
Time Tables

Free Stopover at Niagara Falls

Thru Service
between
Chicago
Cleveland
Buffalo
Scranton, Newark
and
New York
St. Louis {Cleveland
{Toledo
Toledo, Indianapolis

A classic engineer pose as Carl Childs keeps a steady hand on 175.

Steam veteran meets replacement Alco PA "Bluebird" 187, leading the
CITY OF CLEVELAND eastbound for Buffalo.

A water stop was made at Angola, NY.

(Above) *The firebox of 175 taken near Dunkirk.*

(Right) *Looking back along the tender on one of the high bridges of the east end.*

(Above) *Fireman Edward Green has just taken over the left hand seat for the run to East Cleveland after servicing in Conneaut.*

(Right) *Willis McCaleb provides a unique perspective over the coal bunker during the stop at Erie. His color work at the time was taken with a Kodak Retina III C camera using Kodachrome 10 film.*

(Above) *The Conneaut stop provided railfans a chance to experience one last look at a live steam terminal. The 175 provides the center of attention. All the many appliances of the steam age are still in place and functioning.*

(Below) *The L-1b shuffles to the west end of Conneaut Yard. The Nickel Plate owned eight Hudsons built by Brooks and Lima.*

(Right) *Engineer Leon Speaks poses with his fireman Edward Green for the final dash to Cleveland. Engineman Speaks was considered the fastest man on the Cleveland Division. Somehow the ride wouldn't seem as fast behind an internal combustion locomotive.*

(Below) *The Nickel Plate was a prominent Cleveland company in 1958. The city sponsored an industrial tour in September that included the public touring a new caboose and coach.*

15

Near the end of a memorable run at East Cleveland station.

A forlorn 175 awaits the call that will never come. She was stored with a yard switcher in the Conneaut Roundhouse in this March 1959 view.

December 1959 finds 175 still in the storage line at Conneaut with a sister Hudson and several Berkshires. This engine's story was not yet ended, as the Nickel Plate sold it to the Louisiana Eastern Railroad, a short-lived gravel quarry steam collection of a wealthy rail fan. Unfortunately, this dream was short lived and the 175's fate had merely been delayed. Road Foreman of Engines, James Davin, stands beside the racehorse that ran the memorable farewell.

THE
NICKEL PLATE ROAD
SPECIALIZES

AIR
CONDITIONED

IN FURNISHING
EXCELLENT SERVICE
between
Chicago AND Cleveland
BY DAY • BY NIGHT

Buffalo's location made it an ideal eastern gateway for the Nickel Plate. Ten other major railroads and two industrial lines served the area.

(Opposite page) Westbound NCS-5, The Flying Saucer, leaves Tifft Yard, March 1959.

(Above) Willis on board the Saucer records a listing lake boat and a New York Central caboose hop with Fairbanks Morse Switcher 9132. Buffalo's grain elevators oversee this late winter industrial landscape.

(Below) The GP-7 units pass Nickel Plate's first yard switcher, Alco S2 No. 1, on their way out of town. This engine spent all its 21 NKP years in Buffalo before it was sold to the Akron, Canton and Youngstown Railroad in 1963.

19

(Above) *Abbott Road Yard was used to build westbound trains and had a capacity for 510 cars. December 1959 finds Willis' camera looking eastward at Abbott Yard.*

(Below) *Leaving Buffalo on NS-5 across New York Central tracks.*

(Above) *The westbound Saucer crosses Buffalo Creek about 1:00 P.M., and was expected in St. Louis the next morning. March 1959.*

Two Berkshires break any silence remaining at Northeast, PA in 1957. This particular doubleheader features 779 leading 741 on a westbound by the Buffalo milepost. Nickel Plate doubleheaders were always a treat to watch. Nothing can quite match the thrill of steam ganged up at speed. Fortunately, Willis McCaleb was in town to preserve the moment. The 779 has its own special story, having been the Nickel Plate's last new steam locomotive in May of 1949. It is possible to still visit this engine displayed at Lincoln Park in Lima, Ohio. Before leaving Northeast it should be noted that this was the location of the first Nickel Plate C.T.C. installation in January 1942. A 17 mile section of the Buffalo Division extended between here eastward to Westfield, N.Y.

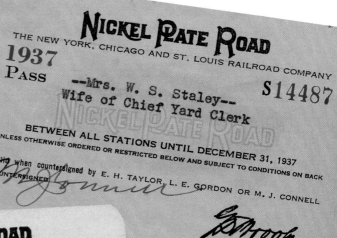

NICKEL PLATE ROAD
THE NEW YORK, CHICAGO AND ST. LOUIS RAILROAD COMPANY
1937
PASS
--Mrs. W. S. Staley--
Wife of Chief Yard Clerk
S14487
BETWEEN ALL STATIONS UNTIL DECEMBER 31, 1937
UNLESS OTHERWISE ORDERED OR RESTRICTED BELOW AND SUBJECT TO CONDITIONS ON BACK
Valid when countersigned by E. H. TAYLOR, L. E. GORDON OR M. J. CONNELL
COUNTERSIGNED
VICE PRESIDENT

NICKEL PLATE ROAD
THE NEW YORK, CHICAGO AND ST. LOUIS RAILROAD COMPANY
1945-46
S12152
PASS
---Mrs. W. S. Staley---
Wife of Chief Yard Clerk-Retired
BETWEEN ALL STATIONS UNTIL DECEMBER 31, 1946
UNLESS OTHERWISE ORDERED OR RESTRICTED BELOW AND SUBJECT TO CONDITIONS ON BACK
VALID WHEN COUNTERSIGNED BY M. J. CONNELL, E. J. BRICKEL OR L. KIMPEL
COUNTERSIGNED
PRESIDENT

(Right) *Skimming along the south shore of Lake Erie, the Nickel Plate reached Erie, PA some 115 miles after leaving Buffalo. Despite the water facilities still in place, steam has been gone for a year and a half. This is January 1960, and the agent at Erie, PA probably has the stove fired up awaiting the next passenger train. We are looking west from the south side of the main line.*

(Below) *The east local from Conneaut to Buffalo graces the landscape near Springfield, PA 1956.*

24 *Willis spent many hours around the railroad's dense facilities at Conneaut, Ohio. One of the road's division points and always a busy terminal, he found many opportunities there for color photography.*

(Above) *The same east local seen at East Springfield is seen earlier in the morning crossing Conneaut Creek. A Mikado heads the peddler while in the background, an eastbound New York Central is pulled by three F's and a GP. The track in the foreground belongs to the Bessemer and Lake Erie Railroad.*

(Right) *Train No. 8 continues from Rocky River Eastbound through Lakewood in 1956. Terminal Tower in downtown Cleveland is 15 minutes away and with the Lackawanna connection in Buffalo, arrives in New York City at 6:55a.m. the next morning.*

Five class C-17 0-8-0's arrived from Lima Locomotive Works, in July of 1934. Two months later came the first Berkshires. Willis remembers when they were brand new, and was in Conneaut to record 304 still at work in 1956.

(Above) *This scene from 1956 could have been posed, but Willis says it "just happened." Men and machines were readied to get the freight over the road, as Berkshire 775 takes on coal for a run to Buffalo. Powerful 0-8-0's 304 and 302 are making up more trains with the yard office on the right.*

(Left) *Caboose 1155 brightens a winter day after being shopped at Conneaut in 1957. This was a classic NKP wooden hack built in 1909.*

Nickel Plate High Speed Service

NICKEL PLATE ROAD

RADIO EQUIPPED

1155

(Above) *The big Berkshire pulls for Buffalo passing the superintendent's office, a Jeep station wagon and a GMC "Cannonball" truck.*

(Below) *On that same 1956 day here is the scene to the west across Chestnut Street. This is the east throat of the Conneaut Yard where eight coupled switchers are still in charge.*

27

(Above) *Switcher 304 crosses West St. between the freight and passenger stations. Round-the-clock use accompanied the purchase of heavy Lima 0-8-0's in the 1930's.*

(Below) *The main line is switched for the Berkshire under the coal tipple in this 1956 view.*

June 1958 finds 746 waiting for a final call on the eastbound ready track.
This engine would make the last steam road haul for the Nickel Plate on
July 2, 1958 with engineer Bill Beard in charge.

ASHTABULA / PAINESVILLE

Willis admits he didn't get out to Ashtabula or Painesville often enough. These results, however, show an appreciation for the famous high bridges of that area.

(Above) A Mike with a 22,000 gallon tender pulls east away from downtown Ashtabula. The spidery bridge rises over a hundred feet above Ashtabula Creek.

NICKEL PLATE SERVICE IS AS NEAR AS YOUR TELEPHONE OR YOUR TWX TELETYPE

NICKEL PLATE ROAD
system map

Freight Traffic Offices are Located in the Cities Shown Below

Albany, New York
Atlanta, Georgia
Baltimore, Maryland
Cleveland, Ohio
Columbus, Ohio
Birmingham, Alabama
Dallas, Texas
Boston, Massachusetts
Davenport, Iowa
Buffalo, New York
Denver, Colorado
Canton, Ohio
Detroit, Michigan
Chicago, Illinois
Erie, Pennsylvania
Cincinnati, Ohio
Lafayette, Indiana
Fort Wayne, Indiana
Los Angeles, California
Grand Rapids, Michigan
Louisville, Kentucky
Houston, Texas
Memphis, Tennessee
Indianapolis, Indiana
Milwaukee, Wisconsin
Kansas City, Missouri
Minneapolis, Minnesota
Pittsburgh, Pennsylvania
Muncie, Indiana
Portland, Oregon
New Orleans, Louisiana
St. Louis, Missouri
New York, New York
Salt Lake City, Utah
Omaha, Nebraska
San Francisco, California
Peoria, Illinois
Seattle, Washington
Philadelphia, Pennsylv
Shreveport, Louisiana
Toledo, Ohio
Tulsa, Oklahoma
Washington, D. C.
Wheeling, West Virginia

Speed your freight
ship Nickel Plate

GENERAL OFFICES, TERMINAL TOWER, CLEVELAND 1, OHIO

Two GP9's lead a westbound over the Grand River at Painesville in June 1958. NKP bought 102 GP9's from 1955 until 1959.

(Above) *Berkshire 746 is captured in color at Painesville after Willis had taken a black and white shot. The NKP is famous for its willowy steel viaducts on the east end of the railroad.*

(Below) *Signal Maintainer, Vincent Murphy stands by his International truck at Painesville in September 1958.*

Caboose 407 brings up the rear of 746's train above Ohio Route 84. The 407 was a 1955 product of the Ironville shops at Toledo, Ohio.

Willis McCaleb and the Nickel Plate made Cleveland both headquarters and home. Willis' assignments reflected the variety of location with special emphasis on the industrial environment. Safety programs provided opportunities to photograph equipment and the people at work.

(Above) *Husky 814 approaches Broadway with CC-2 from Bellevue. Clearly visible are the fills and viaducts needed for the terminal tower project. This is a bright blue day in March 1958.*

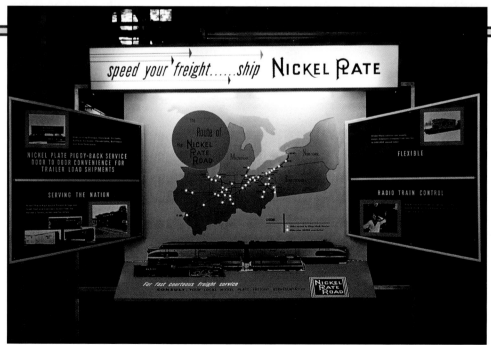

1956 finds the Nickel Plate still promoting passenger service. This store display in Cleveland proudly advances speedy freight service and equipment improvements. Berkshire steam engines are still at the table.

(Right) *Summer 1957 finds H-5b 964 pausing at East 75th Street. Originally built as 522 in 1917, this old Brooks engine would continue to serve for another year.*

(Below) *Willis used the 964 for a series of safety photos to illustrate the "Do's and Don'ts." Here, the fireman demonstrates cistern cover practice at East 75th Street in 1957.*

(Left and Above) *The east local slips under East 55th Street. The ex-Wheeling Berk looks right at home in this industrial setting. Berkshire 802 is the only steam engine Willis operated and that happened in Norwalk Yard. He also rode the engine from Bellevue to Cleveland on another occasion.*

(Below) *964 steams quietly as the crew waits for direction on the next safety shot. Willis refers to this opportunity as "afterthoughts of safety slides," at East 75th Street in 1957.*

NORTHERN OHIO FOOD TERMINAL

Northern Ohio Food Terminal provided Nickel Plate with a major revenue source. Some of the "yellow-bellies" on those famous reefer trains ended up at this huge Cleveland facility. These photos are from the sixties near the end of the food chain for railroads.

We Meet in the Salad Bowl

According to Willis, the first piggy back shipment on the NKP was from Lincoln Electric traveling Cleveland to Chicago. East 9th Street Freight House was the main Cleveland pig yard.

(Above) *Two trailers look toward Terminal Tower in August 1959. Nickel Plate was an early leader in the piggyback business, so early that it was very common to see Nickel Plate truck traffic hauled behind fast moving steam.*

(Below) *Euclid trucks provided a colorful load to a Nickel Plate consist. Summer 1957 finds a "Big Euc" at the Euclid Plant on a new NKP flat car.*

(Above) *Express traffic is up on this early March morning of 1958. No. 7 will make a brief stop at the terminal and then continue west.*

(Below) *This is not the fantrip of May 1958, but probably the power for a baseball excursion. Bumped off regular main line assignments by Alco PA's, the 175 is being turned on the Erie turntable at East 55th Street in the summer of 1956.*

Alco S-2 40 roams about the coach yard in July 1963, keeping company with the famous Civil War veteran, the General. April 1958 still finds a variety of coaches in the yard waiting assignment including company heavyweights, diners, and even some assorted equipment from the United States Army. The ever present Alco switcher presides over movements. In a year, passenger trains will begin their decline, and bring less variety to the coach yard.

NICKEL PLATE ROAD

PASSENGER SCHEDULES
CHANGE OF TIME
SEPTEMBER 25, 1949
Destroy Previous Issues

NICKEL PLATE PASSENGER DIESEL

(Above) *3rd OB-2 crosses the Cuyahoga Valley viaduct eastbound with reefers bound for east coast markets. The "word" around the railroad in those days as Willis remembers it was that each train of perishables was valued at a million dollars.*

(Below) *Willis' camera could find subjects without Nickel Plate subjects such as this splendid view of the industrial Cuyahoga River demonstrates.*

Another OB-2 crosses over new Innerbelt freeway construction in 1956.

Although he was not fond of heights, Willis found himself atop the west tower of the lift bridge at milepost 184.50. MB-98 is eastbound meeting the more sedate Wheeling transfer. In the distance, Willis's 1953 blue Ford can be seen parked on University Road. This is June 1959.

(Left) *Aboard an eastbound puller near East 34th Street enroute to East 55th, a trio of GP-7's approaches in this March 1958 view. The water tank is still active, but not for long.*

(Below) *GP-9's are westbound at the coach yard, April 1958. The road numbered its GP7's 400-447 and its GP9's 448-543 with an additional 15 numbered 800-814.*

(Left) *Built in 1883 and still bouncing behind main line merchandise, a cold, gloomy 1957 day finds caboose 1062 crossing the Cuyahoga Valley. Waiting for the caboose to pass was one of the great traditions of railroading. There was always a smile and a friendly wave.*

Three views of action at Cloggville on the near west side of Cleveland.

(Top) *This winter scene includes the Leisy Brewery just left of the bridge. February 1958 finds 727 taking a westbound over the almost new Cleveland Rapid Transit. The Berkshire will be laid up in June 1958.*

(Center and bottom) *Eastbound OB-2 is escorted over the Big Four Railroad by GP-9s and an Alco RS-11. This train preceded the steam freight on the same June day in 1958. Transition was almost complete.*

(Opposite page) *No. 10 from St. Louis slips by the West 98th Street Rapid Transit Station. The spur track leads to the Neal Storage building.*

WEST 98th STREET

The parallel Cleveland Rapid Transit Station at West 98th Street was a great location to get close to Nickel Plate run bys.

(Left) Here, Mike 530 wheels by in the summer of 1955. This engine will be renumbered 968 in December, it still has a couple years left before retirement.

(Below) Willis is on the platform waiting for the Rapid when No. 10 appears. John Fox, Road Foreman of Engines for the Cleveland Division, acknowledges the "official photographer" of the Nickel Plate from the engine door.

(Above) *Two GP-9s and one GP-7 begin their run through Lakewood just west of 117th Street in May 1958.*

(Below) *Cleveland Union Terminal is twenty minutes away with PA-1 182 pulling across Rocky River in April 1958. No. 10 left St. Louis the previous evening.*

ROCKY RIVER

(Opposite page) *The Rocky River is a north-south waterway extending from Medina county to Lake Erie. This double track NKP viaduct across the Rocky River provided a dramatic setting for many of Willis' pictures since his home was close by. Spring 1958 still finds a Berkshire eastbound on CC-2.*

(Above) *Three Electro-Motive GPs pull eastbound in April 1958.*

(Below) *Looking down from the Westlake Hotel high above the viaduct and the finish of a westbound freight with wooden veteran 1155. The Westlake is a local landmark, once a hotel now converted to condominiums.*

(Above) *On a clear day you can see the Avon Power Plant from the Westlake Hotel and on this March day in 1958, the morning local, No. 91, stops at Rocky River. The depot became a favorite subject for Willis. He became fast friends with the operators, and it was their cooperation that made many of the pictures around the station possible.*

(Right) *The east side of the depot catches the morning sun in 1956.*

Looks like No. 8 is late. Anxious passengers gaze into the sun as PA-1 182 draws the New York bound train into Rocky River. Most of the people are waiting for No. 9, which is due from downtown Cleveland about 6:15 P.M. in the summer of 1956.

The CITY OF ERIE glides by following a diner lounge. Tacked on the back of No. 8 are three heavy-weights. This could be a baseball excursion bound for a night game at Municipal Stadium. The fans would come home on No. 5. Note the red 1952 De Soto convertible parked alongside the depot.

Right on time is No. 9 arriving from downtown. The 185 leads the way as the boarding passengers anticipate which coach door will open. Orders are in place for an eastbound and shortly, a 700 bears down from the west. Young and old peer into the sun to reap the reward of hanging around the depot on the Nickel Plate in 1956.

(Above) *All trains stopped at Rocky River, so it became a favorite subject for Willis. A friendly environment provided a loyal group of passenger patrons. Some were commuters, but many were just visiting friends and relatives out along the line. The train for St. Louis began in Cleveland at 6:00 P.M. Overnight it called on Fostoria, Lima, Muncie, Frankfort, Charleston, and finally, 6:45 A.M., St. Louis. Here, once again, No. 9 arrives to take care of the faithful in 1956.*

(Left) *Even the cream cans got respect from the NKP.*

Soon after 8:00 in the morning, No. 10 arrives at Rocky River from St. Louis. Always a modest consist with light traffic, the train is easily handled by one PA 1. May 1958. Nickel Plate passenger cars always had interesting murals and decor. Here is a fine map from one of the business cars. Willis captured it August of 1959 in the Cleveland Coach Yard.

(Above) *No. 6, the CITY OF CLEVELAND, thrusts its nose into the morning air. Due at Rocky River at 6:41 A.M., the train had left Chicago the previous evening at 10:20. The 185 looks very good in the early light and Willis was there that day in May, 1958.*

(Right) *Running on the Buffalo Division out of Conneaut, is engineer Edward Ryan at the controls. Willis was on board this PA 1 in November 1959.*

(Above) *Willis has approached the trestle to find the usual brace of PAs on No 7, the morning train to Chicago. April 1958.*

(Below) *Rocky River Station at night, open for business. Snow tops this study in December 1959. Maybe the operator will let us warm up inside and hang around for No. 5.*

(Left) *Denny Morris was 2nd trick operator at Rocky River and Willis's favorite "OP." It was through his friendship and cooperation that many of these pictures were accomplished. "A modest little guy who just worked his job and was accommodating to the serious fans that came by."*

(Below) *March 1958 finds ex-Wheeling 810 still with CC-2. The train will lose its symbol at Cleveland, and become the east local to Conneaut. Steam was diminishing with each day and Rocky River was a great location to witness its final parade.*

The Cleveland Flats host 500 guests of the railroad community committee in May 1956. A twelve-car train traveled over the tracks of Erie, Nickel Plate and New York Central. Box lunches are being passed out at the Erie Ore Docks.

Nickel Plate dining car bib based on a painting by Howard Fogg for the American Locomotive Company.

NICKEL PLATE ROAD

Willis and his father, Earl, came upon an eastbound switching the Sheffield Yard in June 1958. This was very late for main line steam, but it provided Willis with one last opportunity to document a working 700.

(Right) An engineman exits an Alco Road Switcher in March 1960.

(Below) Earl McCaleb waits for Willis in the '53 Ford. "The car needs a wash, but I put 113,000 miles on it."

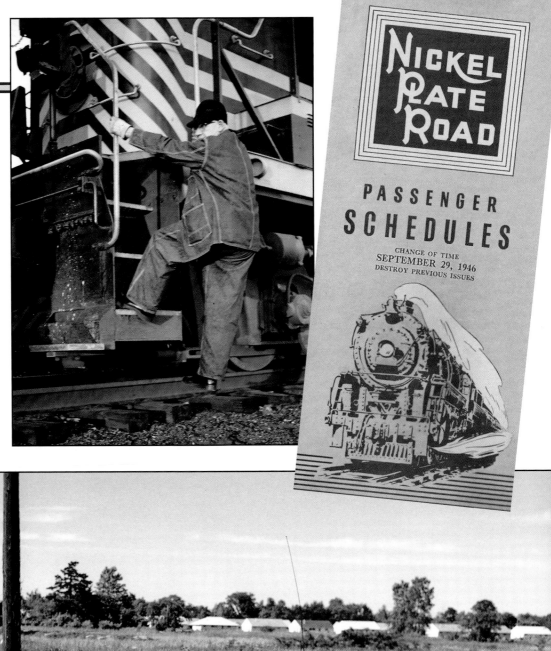

NICKEL PLATE ROAD

PASSENGER SCHEDULES

CHANGE OF TIME
SEPTEMBER 29, 1946
DESTROY PREVIOUS ISSUES

Showing off some of her best features, 763 faces a bright afternoon sun. In a few days, this engine will join others in Conneaut and remain under steam until July 22, when the Nickel Plate dropped the fires on all the big engines. This series by Willis illustrates the wonderful drama created by an ordinary switching move during the steam age.

(Left) *A Berkshire from the rear is a load. 763 pulls across a local road to access the switch showing the immense tender to good advantage.*

(Below and opposite page) *Soon, the engine couples to a string of chemical tank cars pulling them from the B.F. Goodrich Plant.*

(Above) *Switching stops as the eastbound No. 8 glides by from Chicago. PA-1 181 will be in Cleveland Terminal by 5:30 P.M.*

(Below) *Engine, tanks and others head westbound for Bellevue. Ahead lies 46 miles of flat running.*

PIGGY-BACK SERVICE

Nickel Plate started to put truck trailers on flat cars in July 1954, which was very early in piggy-back service. Boxcars were converted to flats at Conneaut in early 1959. Willis was there to record new flats recently converted from boxcars and trailers at the Fruehauf Trailer Plant in Avon Lake, Ohio in March 1959.

Announcing...

Nickel Plate trailer-flatcar
"PIGGY-BACK" SERVICE

between

Chicago • Philadelphia • Baltimore

(Above) *A line up of new trailers and flats stand at the Fruehauf Plant. The new orange trailers belong to the Lackawanna.*

(Below) *Anyone passing through Cleveland Union Terminal in the early 1960's might remember this backlighted sign promoting the service. The innovation was a success and provided extra loads for the road in 1961 and the years to follow.*

May 1958 finds the water tank at South Lorain still intact but without business. Lorain is 26 miles west of Cleveland and was a junction with the Lorain and West Virginia running to Wellington, Ohio.

Hudson 174 in work train service in central Lorain, not the usual duty for a classy passenger engine, but by 1956 any employment was welcome. Laid up in 1958, but later sold to the Louisiana Eastern along with 173 and 175, alas they did not survive.

EQUIPMENT

No. 5—CITY OF CHICAGO—Daily

Sleeping Cars (Roomettes-Double Bedrooms)
Buffalo to Chicago
Cleveland to Chicago (Open 10.00 P.M.)
Reclining Seat Coaches
New York and Buffalo to Chicago
Dining Service
New York to Hornell
Club-Diner-Lounge
Cleveland to Chicago (Open 10.00 P.M.)
(Via Erie-Lackawanna No. 1-31 New York to Buffalo)

No. 6—CITY OF CLEVELAND—Daily

Sleeping Cars (Roomettes-Double Bedrooms)
Chicago to Cleveland and Buffalo
(Open at Chicago at 10.00 P.M.)
Reclining Seat Coaches
Chicago to Buffalo (Open 10.30 P.M.)
Club-Diner-Lounge
Chicago to Cleveland (Open 10.00 P.M.)

No. 7—THE WESTERNER—Daily

Sleeping Cars (Roomettes-Double Bedrooms)
New York to Cleveland
Reclining Seat Coaches
New York and Buffalo to Chicago
Diner
New York to Hornell
Diner Lounge
Buffalo to Chicago
(Via Erie-Lackawanna No. 5-35 New York to Buffalo)

No. 8—THE NEW YORKER—Daily

Sleeping Cars (Roomettes-Double Bedrooms)
Cleveland to New York
Reclining Seat Coaches
Chicago to Buffalo and New York
Diner Lounge
Chicago to Buffalo
Diner
Hornell to New York
(Via Erie-Lackawanna No. 36-6 Buffalo to New York)

(Left) *Willis rides the last run of No. 8 through Lorain in June of 1963.*

(Below) *Late Berkshire action eastbound along Lake Erie, west of Lorain in 1958. Although the Van Sweringen Berkshires were operated on Chesapeake and Ohio, Pere Marquette and Erie, as well as the NKP, the Nickel Plate was the last to operate this very successful breed.*

KISHMANS

Always a troublesome point on the Cleveland Division because of dense traffic, but little more than a wide spot on the railroad, Kishmans is 8 miles west of Lorain at the end of double-track.

(Below) Hot Summer 1956 at KM (Kishmans). The 763 hammers eastbound on June 26, 1956.

Willis found a westbound coming off the double track at Kishmans. CTC was installed during 1942 to help ease the traffic bottleneck over this busy stretch of railroad west of Cleveland. Big 771 takes to the single track for the dash to Bellevue on June 26, 1956 as steam is still in charge of most main line freights.

GC TOWER

West of Vermilion sits a concrete block building identified by the Nickel Plate as GC Tower. A water tank and CTC sidings take up most of the landscape. This tower also controlled the siding at KM. In this McCaleb classic, June afternoon traffic includes Mike 662 at GC. The Lima H-6 lasted in the Cleveland-Bellevue service until April 1958.

BUF 222

The same June day sees another H-6, 647, back past GC, stand next to the water plug, and finally move west toward Bellevue. Willis ran across this action in 1956.

FRIES LANDING

The morning train to Chicago crosses the Huron River at Fries Landing. After No. 7 clears, a work extra quickly follows. Hudson 174 may have preferred the passenger assignment, but work is hard to find in 1956.

NICKEL PLATE ROAD

Old Route 299 crossed the Nickel Plate near Avery on the Cleveland Division. Willis stood on the bridge to record two trains on two different days.

(Right) 2-8-2 651 runs for Cleveland on an extra in 1956.

(Below) Wooden cab 1140 trails tank cars westbound in 1957. This caboose was built in 1881 in Lafayette, Indiana.

PORT
OF
HURON
OHIO

COAL AND
ORE DOCKS

THE WHEELING AND LAKE ERIE
RAILWAY COMPANY

HURON BRANCH

(Above) *In 1875, the Wheeling and Lake Erie took advantage of the collapse of the Milan Canal, and eventually created a line to the lake port of Huron. Iron ore tonnage pulling upgrade from Lake Erie could be spectacular, however on a quiet late winter afternoon in 1957, Alco 818 drifts by "Lover's Lane" with the Norwalk-Huron turn.*

(Opposite page) *Giant Hulett unloaders extract Minnesota ore from the hold of the steamer ERNEST T. WEIR. The coal and ore docks could be a busy port during the shipping season. Ore was removed for the mills around Steubenville and coal from southern Ohio was loaded onto the lake boats. This activity was enhanced by grain business from an elevator across the slip from the ore dock. There was also an interchange with the New York Central. Never a dull day in Huron and Willis was there in August 1962.*

(Above) *Berkshire 803 basks in the summer sun, perhaps dreaming of her early days as Wheeling 6403.*

(Below) *2-8-4 772 escorts a load of pipe in 1956.*

Imagine having to simply stop and shoot live working steam locomotives anytime it was convenient. Willis had just that opportunity during 1956 at the engine facility in Norwalk, Ohio. These locomotives services the Huron Branch for ore train service.

(Above) *Keeping company with Lima 0-8-0 225 and Brooks 2-8-2 959, Willis' father stands by the 803.*

(Below) *Another Lima switcher shows a white feather at Norwalk.*

Norwalk's roundhouse will soon be without live steam, but on this glorious day in 1956, all is well. Steam and cinders abound with Berk 816 ready to take on Hartland Hill one more time.

(Above) *225 pauses by the water tank with Norwalk's yard on the right.*

(Below) *Willis takes a low perspective on the only steam engine he ever ran, ex W&LE 802. He was allowed to move it around the Norwalk yard. Willis' comment on viewing these photos again almost forty years later, "Can you imagine what a lot of fun all this was?"*

(Above) *Lima 219 is readied as a hostler sees to her needs. One of the company's International panel trucks is on the right.*

Switchers stare at each other in 1957 and steam on the Wheeling will soon be gone. Acquired by the Nickel Plate in 1949, the W&LE was a valuable asset to the Nickel Plate contributing substantial ore and coal tonnage.

Willis is aboard the caboose of No. 89 as two GPs pull No. 90 eastbound at Norwalk in 1957.

MONROEVILLE

(Left) *Wheeling and Lake Erie interchanged with the Baltimore and Ohio at Monroeville a few miles west of Norwalk. August 1956 finds ex W&LE 272 attached to ex W&LE caboose 885 moving among the switches.*

(Below) *On another day, the 0-8-0 teams with 911, another Wheeling cab. This was the "puller" between Norwalk and Bellevue. "Puller" was a local term for transfer freight.*

THE NEW YORK, CHICAGO AND ST. LOUIS RAILROAD COMPANY

OFFICE OF THE PRESIDENT

TERMINAL TOWER · CLEVELAND 1, OHIO

Nickel Plate High Speed Service
NICKEL PLATE ROAD 1157

CLEVELAND
SEP 11
7 30PM
1953
OHIO

U.S. POSTAGE
AMOUNT
.03
PAID
P.B. METER 56008

Mr. Willis A. McCaleb,
Photographer,
Nickel Plate Road,
Cleveland, Ohio.

MAIN 1-9000

NICKEL PLATE ROAD

WILLIS A. McCALEB

432 TERMINAL TOWER

CLEVELAND, O.

WILLIS A. McCALEB
SIGNATURE OF MEMBER

PHOTOGRAPHER CLEVELAND
TITLE   LOCATION

1882-1951

The New York, Chicago & St. Louis Railroad Company
NICKEL PLATE
V25V
ASSOCIATION

Thirty-Fourth Annual Convention

OF

The
Veteran
Association of

NICKEL PLATE ROAD

AT

CEDAR POINT
OHIO

AUGUST 18th, 1951

NICKEL PLATE

ROUND TABLE CLUB

50th Annual Banquet

the Manger Hotel · Saturday, January *19, 1963*

Steam locomotives lived long useful lives, especially on the Nickel Plate. Bellevue engine terminal was very efficient, so not many locos sat around long. They were out earning their keep, working on the many east and westbound manifests or several locals that Bellevue originated. In the mid fifties, while most other railroad's terminals were lined with stored steam for scrap, the NKP dispatched its hottest freight with the speedy Berkshires. Willis spent many hours in Bellevue not just for his job assignments, but to spend some personal time with a still very active steam terminal. Being a railroad employee allowed him to reach parts of the terminal not otherwise available by the safety conscious NKP.

Limas dominate the landscape on this summer afternoon in 1956. H-6 639 first takes a turn under the 500 ton coal dock, then moves up next to 774 on the eastbound ready track. A hostler looks after the Mike, which will be donated to Bloomington, Illinois in 1959.

Bellevue had a good share of passenger train activity. Steam and Alco PAs complemented each other six times a day during the 1950's. Here Willis leans out the vestibule of No. 8 to catch 751 getting out of town on a westbound, in June 1957.

(Above) *Alcos pull No. 8 away from the depot and past a still steamy service area.*

(Below) *2-8-2 954 attaches business car No. 6 to the back of an eastbound in April 1958.*

Lima Berkshire 765 looks as handsome as ever riding the Bellevue turntable in 1957. This would have been a fitting finale for most reciprocating steam locomotives looking for one more assignment in the late 1950's. The 765 survives in the 1990's as a tribute to the solid engineering and good design decisions made decades ago by Lima and the Nickel Plate.

BELLEVUE ROUNDHOUSE

Willis never enjoyed heights, but some of his most interesting work comes from above. "We were nutty enough to do it once" was Willis' comment when reviewing this session. "I didn't do this for the company, but thought it would make for some interesting perspectives and be quite different from the usual ground shots." 2-8-4 727 was still under steam in May 1958. An obliging hostler pulls the engine onto the table for one last portrait. The 727 was built by Lima in July 1942. Sixteen years old, and with only a few more miles to run, she was laid up at Bellevue on June 23 and not scrapped until 1961.

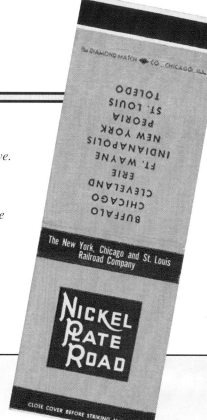

As 727 eases back to the roundhouse stall after her photo shoot, the background reveals 810 and 954 retired as of May 8, 1958. GP-9 482 will survive into the 1990's as Indiana and Ohio #65.

Willis much preferred the old roundhouses to the modern Bellevue facility, but he always seemed to bring out the best in the concrete and glassblock structure.

(Above) *Wheeling switcher 5119 was renumbered NKP 289, and last ran at Brewster in 1956. It was a 1930 product of W&LE.*

(Right) *H-5 507 came from Lima in April 1917. Renumbered 954, this engine was often assigned to the Narlo Stone Run and work extras.*

From his lofty climb atop the roundhouse, Willis finds a willing subject in Berkshire 763. Still in steam in May 1958, she would remain ready until all fires were dropped July 22, 1958.

(Above) *The yard is empty of steam activity, and the ready tracks are populated with striped diesels. The 763 puts up a good front, but transition is almost complete.*

(Right) *A bemused engineman eases west and looks up at Willis on high.*

(Above) *Even GP-9s caught Willis' attention on top of the roundhouse. The functional 522 and 461 ride the table on this May day.*

Safety inspector, Waldo Richards and Willis McCaleb share the moment and prove they were there, May 24, 1958. (Photo: Paul J. Kick)

(Left) *Operator controls movements at the Bellevue Yard in April 1963.*

(Above) *Alco RS-11 573 was the first new unit delivered in the new wide stripe paint scheme. Rain and sun have bleached the soot from the roundhouse.*

(Below) *One of Willis' attempts at glamorizing the house. "The only way you could make that Bellevue roundhouse look good was using it for a frame." EMDs and Alcos have taken up residence. June 1961.*

(Above) *The occasion can't be identified, but it looks like a retirement for the man in the bright flowered shirt. A PA-1 forms the backdrop for the engine house force on this August day 1961. Lots of stories could be told here.*

(Left) *One of the many dramas of steam railroading was replacing tires on engine drivers. Willis captured this timeless scene at the engine house in 1956.*

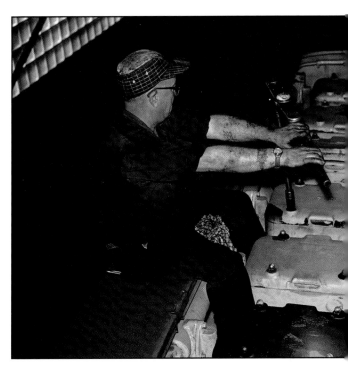

(Left and above) *Safety shots were not glamorous but they did show excellent detail. One of the engine house crew climbs on the 770 with all the attending grime in April 1958. Diesel maintenance could also generate dirt as a mechanic works on a cylinder head in the Bellevue house in 1956.*

(Below) *Another of the existing 700s rides the table in 1957. A visit to the railroad museum in Conneaut will find the engine today.*

Corporate color photography was not common in the 1950's, and Willis wonders, "Why did I wait so long?" Part of the problem was that he had to rent a camera and it wasn't a priority. Besides, film was slow and railroading could be very fast.

(Above) *The eastbound ready track is crowded with 700s waiting for the evening parade of manifests. Forty or more trains left Bellevue daily, so this power won't sit very long. The gentleman in the fedora appears to be leading a symphony of steam. First engine out is 746, which would take the last run for steam road power in July 1958.*

(Opposite page top) *Another road warrior takes a turn under the coal dock. "Triple sevens" won't be lucky for long as she has zebra stripes on her heels in April 1958 and only two months remain.*

(Opposite page bottom) *When the original Berkshire was delivered in 1934, there was hope this new class would pull the company through the depression, bringing speed and efficiency. Twenty-two years later, that first engine sits under the brooding coal dock with fire on the grates. The pioneering 700 will run one more year. 1956 was a good year indeed to check the horses on the ready tracks.*

(Left) *Alco RS-11 560 stands under a coal dock it doesn't need in October 1959. Filling the sanders has left the ground looking like a beach. This unit was off the property after only 12 years. Color photography of Nickel Plate's all diesel years (1958-1964) is somewhat limited since the company merged so soon after D-Day.*

(Right) *Checking the orders for another road haul in October 1959.*

(Below) *A 700 livens up the flat plain that was Bellevue yard. Steam made a statement whether near or far in 1956.*

NICKEL PLATE ROAD

NICKEL PLATE HIGH SPEED SERVICE

ROUTING CHART

Routing Chart showing service routes for carload traffic between stations in Western Trunk Line, Southwestern, Inter-Mountain and Trans-Continental territories and points in the following states located on railroads shown in this chart:

CONNECTICUT	MASSACHUSETTS	
DELAWARE	MICHIGAN	RHODE ISLAND
ILLINOIS	NEW HAMPSHIRE	VERMONT
INDIANA	NEW JERSEY	VIRGINIA
KENTUCKY	NEW YORK	WEST VIRGINIA
MAINE	OHIO	WISCONSIN
MARYLAND	PENNSYLVANIA	CANADA (EASTERN)

Routes shown in this chart apply via St. Louis, Mo., East St. Louis, Ill., Chicago, Ill., or Peoria, Ill., unless otherwise indicated in the individual routes shown herein. These routes are generally applicable on both eastbound and westbound, or northbound and southbound traffic with few exceptions. (From and to Western Trunk Line, Inter-Mountain and Trans-Continental Territories on traffic moving via Chicago, Ill., routes are also applicable via Cheneyville, Ill., except as otherwise provided.)

TRUCK TRAFFIC

1958 ended main line steam, but it also saw a major push among all railroads to haul highway trailers on flat cars. Nickel Plate saw the future early, converting flat cars and buying trailers. Bellevue originated some of this traffic. On the same day Willis photographed steam from the roundhouse roof, he found an eastbound with trailers, May 24, 1958.

Open top trailers ride on Santa Fe flats at Bellevue. Nickel Plate marked their trailers with the familiar company logo or in this case a very spartan "NKP" on the ends. The aluminum box on the left, however, carries full Nickel Plate identification in this November 1961 view.

1958 was not only a benchmark for fans of the Nickel Plate, but also the crews. Life in the profession was changing. Not everyone would miss the hard work of steam, but most took pride in their handling of locomotives and getting the freight over the division. Willis recalls fondly his encounter with two proud steam veterans, engineer Forrest Hosler and fireman Cecil Quackenbush. They were taking the big Lima, 764, westbound to Ft. Wayne.

Willis summarizes:
"They were a couple of neat guys."

The engine has two months of service left. Engineer Hosler oils around, even though yard switchers surround the engine.

764

April 1958 still saw a few 700s dispatched east and west from Bellevue.
Fortunately, Willis found an opportunity to document what it was all about.
Neat guys, neat engines, neat pictures.

A stark winter landscape gives a perfect stage for a 700 in full flight, east of Bellevue from Route 113. Sometimes, a distant perspective told the story more effectively. Ohio's flatland was part of the reason for the long success of Nickel Plate steam. Gentle grades and tangent track were perfect for high speed service behind the big-wheeled Berks.

During Willis' pursuit of NKP steam during the late 1950's, it was difficult not to notice another part of the Bellevue rail scene. Pennsylvania's Columbus to Sandusky line was busy and very steamy.

(Above) *Southbound behind the roundhouse stands J-1 6478. Powerful, but handsome, and reflecting the Pennsy's knack for style. Summer has brought grass and weeds to the rails. This summer of 1957 has also brought diesels, and by season's end this 2-10-4 will be laid up for good.*

NICKEL PLATE ROAD

THE NEW YORK, CHICAGO AND ST. LOUIS RAILROAD COMPANY

NICKLE PLATE ROAD

CIRCUS TRAIN NO. SIX

TIMETABLE

INDIANAPOLIS TO PERU

AUGUST 11, 1962

One year earlier and the famous summer of 1956 brought the huge 2-10-4s from the Santa Fe to assist the almost retired J-1s. Imagine waiting for No. 8 at the depot, when suddenly the mass of 5022 eases southbound with empties. Even the crew of Fairbanks Morse switcher 129 gives it some attention. Willis camera gives us a glimpse of that special time.

In 1956 a visit to Bellevue yard could be taken for granted that one would find mostly steam. Berkshires took most freights out of town in all directions. Here, 738 escorts a manifest westbound past Bellevue depot and beanery.

POWER TRANSITION

(Above) *Fewer assignments were found for steam in 1957, but 763 has an eastbound extra in tow.*

(Below) *All steam is stored by 1960 as Alco 562 brings a string of units west to the service area. They won't be needing coal.*

At the control stand of GP-9 460, as sister 461 peers out of the roundhouse in June 1961.

(Above) *All the crew is on the porch of 451 arriving from Toledo.*

(Below) *Two road switchers pose under a tank in steamless June 1961. The Nickel Plate never acquired F7 cab units for its freights.*

Jack O'Neil, (seated) Freight Agent at Bellevue, poses for a moment on the occasion of his retirement as a railroader. Willis captures the pride and hard work that came with the profession, May 1959.

Fairbanks Morse switcher 145 appears somewhat disheveled, pulling a tidy string of new Akron, Canton and Youngstown freight cars. 1966 dates this scene and the merger is two years past. No. 145 will become N&W 2145 the next year. Nickel Plate probably wouldn't have allowed the unit to look so shabby. This switcher type was the last purchased by the NKP. Their order in 1958 were the final Fairbanks diesels built for domestic use. Transition was more than coal to diesels. It was a change of paint liveries, a change of management and shift away from the familiar.

Willis provides an interesting perspective to filling the sanders on GP-9 503 under the coal dock, October 1959.

(Above) *EMD GP-9 457 occupies the same space Berkshire 763 had 2 years before. May 1959.*

(Left) *An imposing view of Alco 562 illustrates a safety point concerning the brake wheel. Those wide front end stripes provided Nickel Plate with another unique identity at Bellevue, November 1960.*

Clearance Specialist, Clarence Kirch, steps out of the cab of passenger GP-9 485 at Bellevue. This is the last day for train No. 8.

The last run of the NEW YORKER was June 2, 1963. Willis took the WESTERNER, No. 7, to Ft. Wayne in order to ride the final No. 8 back to Cleveland. He was assigned to help a television cameraman cover the demise of Nickel Plate passenger service. Highway travel had blunted even the most loyal NKP passenger and stories of the diminishing trains became a popular news story.

NICKEL PLATE ROAD

CHICAGO • CLEVELAND • BUFFALO • NEW YORK

EASTBOUND Read down				WESTBOUND Read up	
City of Cleveland No. 6 Daily	The New Yorker No. 8 Daily	Miles	SPECIAL NOTICE Train No. 7, Buffalo to Chicago, and Train No. 8, Chicago to Buffalo are subject to discontinuance under Application pending before the Interstate Commerce Commission. Consult agent prior to date of travel.	The Westerner No. 7 Daily	City of Chicago No. 5 Daily
PM 10.30	AM 9.50		Lv Chicago Central Standard Time .... Ar	PM 3.55	AM 6.50
			CENTRAL DAYLIGHT TIME		
*11.30	*10.50	0.0	Lv Chicago (LaSalle St. Sta.), Ill. .... Ar	4.55	7.50
p 11.44	p 11.04	6.7	Englewood (59 W. 63rd St.) Lv	p 4.40	p 7.33
12.11	11.33	19.9	Hammond, Ind.	3.54	6.38
g 12.25	g 11.45	30.6	South Gary (Gary) ▲	z 3.33	z 6.18
	k 12.01	46.5	Valparaiso		m 5.59
1.13	12.23	72.0	Knox	2.51	5.36
a 1.26	a 12.42	84.8	Hibbard ▲	a 2.34	a 5.19
		92.2	Argos ▲ (CDT)		
			EASTERN STANDARD TIME		
		112.7	Claypool ▲		
	w 1.24	126.5	South Whitley	w 1.49	4.37
2.41	1.55	152.2	Ar Fort Wayne, Ind. Lv	1.22	4.10
2.56	2.00	152.2	Lv Fort Wayne, Ind. Ar	1.10	3.50
	e 2.22	174.0	Payne, Ohio	n 12.43	
		181.5	Latty		
u 3.48	2.46	198.0	Continental	12.17	x 2.38
c 4.07		213.0	Leipsic Jct.	v 12.01	x 2.21
	3.10	222.9	McComb	w 11.49	
c 4.27	3.22	230.5	North Findlay (Sta. for Findlay)	11.40	1.57
4.51	3.42	243.1	Rostoria	11.25	1.38
	b 4.01	263.4	Green Springs		
5.30	4.15	275.6	Ar Bellevue Lv	10.49	1.01
5.35	4.18	275.6	Lv Bellevue (EST) Ar	10.45	12.56
			EASTERN DAYLIGHT TIME		
		302.3	Vermilion ▲		
7.23	6.03	313.0	Lorain	11.03	1.09
7.45	6.25	331.0	Rocky River (Lakewood)	10.40	12.40
8.10	6.50	339.7	Ar Cleveland (Union Terminal) Lv	10.20	12.20
8.30	7.05	339.7	Lv Cleveland (Union Terminal) Ar	10.00	11.55
f 9.03		359.6	Willoughby		
9.20	7.44	369.9	Painesville	9.15	11.12
9.52	8.11	395.6	Ashtabula	8.48	10.45
10.11	8.30	408.7	Ar Conneaut, Ohio Lv	8.29	10.26
10.15	8.35	408.7	Lv Conneaut, Ohio Ar	8.25	10.22
		421.6	Girard, Pa. ▲		
10.55	9.12	436.8	Erie	7.51	9.46
11.11		450.5	North East, Pa.		
f 11.26	h 9.44	466.2	Westfield, N.Y. ▲		
11.45		482.7	Dunkirk		y 9.17
12.40	11.00	523.8	Ar Buffalo (515 Babcock St.), N.Y. (EDT) Lv	*6.15	8.15

Some railroads began to appreciate the machines that made it all possible. Nickel Plate saved several examples including H-6 Mike 639. Last run in 1957, the 2-8-2 was donated to Bloomington, Ill. Seen shortly before a final trip west in September 1959. Original Hudson 170 was given to the Museum of Transport in St. Louis in October 1957. A couple of her class were still active at this time.

(Above) *Wheeling-built 292 was last run in Norwalk yard, October 1957. The iron horse is out to pasture and rusts away in Bellevue, May 1959.*

(Below) *Stored steam engines became a nuisance and were pushed from one storage area to another. The 292 has been shifted in November 1960. This line up in Bellevue yard could be easily seen from eastbound No. 8. It was good to still find some old friends patiently waiting for a call. Finally, by 1962, most were off the property.*

(Right) *Northern Ohio winters can be brutal. A brakeman wrestles with the wheel in the snow in March 1960.*

(Below) *Snow gives the landscape a calming effect, but steam is still alive in Bellevue in 1956.*

NICKEL PLATE ROAD

Volume two of this series will begin with more winter scenes in the yard and move south and west along the NKP.
We invite you to share in more color photography of Willis A. McCaleb and the Nickel Plate Road.